When

Someone

Dies

EDGAR N. JACKSON

Fortress Press   Philadelphia

Copyright © 1971 by Fortress Press

All rights reserved. No part of this publication may be reproduced, stored in a retrieval system, or transmitted in any form or by any means, electronic, mechanical, photocopying, recording, or otherwise, without the prior permission of the copyright owner.

Library of Congress Catalog Card Number 76-154488

ISBN 0-8006-1103-9

Sixth Printing 1984

1069B84   Printed in the United States of America   1-1103

Series

Introduction

Pocket Counsel Books are intended to help people with problems in a specific way. Problems may arise in connection with family life, marriage, grief, alcoholism, drugs or death. In addressing themselves to these and similar problems, the authors have made every effort to speak in language free from technical vocabulary.

Because these books are not only nontechnical but also brief, they offer a good start in helping people with specific problems. Face-to-face conversation between counselor and counselee is a necessary part of the help the authors envision through these books. The books are not a substitute for person-to-person counseling: they supplement counseling.

As the reader gets into a book dealing with his concerns, he will discover that the author aims at opening up areas of inquiry for further reflection. Thus through what is being read that which needs to be said and spoken out loud may come to the surface in dialog with the counselor. In "working through" a given problem in this personal way, help may come.

WILLIAM E. HULME
General Editor

To
Howard C. Raether
and
Robert C. Slater

Contents

1.

The Universal Experience

Everyone knows that death is inevitable. But this common knowledge gives no assurance that we will be prepared for the experience when it comes. In a sense death is the one event for which we can never be fully prepared. Whether we try to anticipate our own death or that of someone we love, our imagination falls short of grasping its total impact.

Part of the difficulty is that no two deaths are ever exactly the same. The experience of death varies according to the way it arrives and the kind of person who faces it. Death may pounce upon us suddenly and without warning. Or it may creep toward us with slow and measured step. Sometimes it comes as a welcome friend after a long period of intolerable suffering. Our reaction will depend in large part on how death makes its appearance.

So also, death does different things to different people. Each of us is a unique individual who must face death in his own special way. The differences in our makeup come out in our dissimilar feelings in response to death. There are, however, certain common reactions that can be described and can lead us toward an understanding of the experience of death.

When the death of someone we love is sudden and tragic we are apt to be overwhelmed by shock and anguish. At first we may be most aware of our grief as a physical reaction. We may feel tightness in the throat and have difficulty in swallowing and speaking.

We may feel waves of discomfort surge back and forth through our bodies for periods ranging from a few minutes to several hours. This discomfort may be hard to describe because it is not like a sharp pain fixed in one spot. It is rather a vague misery that we feel everywhere at once and nowhere in particular.

At times the physical reactions may include shortness of breath and difficulty in breathing. We may seek relief by letting out long and spontaneous sighs. At other times we may feel mild nausea and a strange emptiness in the pit of the stomach.

Or again we may feel weak and faint. Our muscles may seem to have lost their strength. Our arms feel heavy and our feet may not go where we want them to. In fact, our muscles may seem to be out of control, directed by an alien force that can even make them vibrate and shake intensely. We may feel chills followed by hot and cold perspiration. Sometimes our reaction takes the form of a distressing pain that is like a headache, yet not like most headaches because it is so generalized.

These physical reactions to sudden death are not abnormal. This is the way our physical system responds to the shock of life-shattering change. It is not unusual for these symptoms to recur in lesser or greater degree at unexpected times, such as when the name of the dead person is mentioned or sympathy is offered.

Tragic and untimely death produces more than physical effects, however. There are mental and emotional reactions as well. It may seem, for example, that your mind is out of control. Your thoughts may run away with you. Instead of the usual orderly processes that guide your thinking, there may be a pell-mell, helter-skelter jumble of ideas tumbling through your mind. Some of your ideas may express acute anxiety about yourself and your future. Some may express a self-pity which can compound your sadness. Others may reveal a deep anger against life and God and the circumstances that have dealt you a cruel blow.

Your anger and resentment over the injustice of life may for a time overwhelm you. These feelings can also be compounded by guilt that rises up when you think of how different the past might have been. You may be inclined toward a bitterness that colors your attitudes toward other people as well as toward yourself.

In the midst of your pain and confusion you may come to think your intense feelings and wild ideas are somehow "wrong." So you may even be tempted to invent feelings that you think are more valid or appropriate than those you really have. You may want to say and do things that you think others would expect of you.

During a time of such confused feelings it is well to keep in mind that your loss is real, your grief is real, your feelings are a part of you and it is the real feelings that have to be faced and worked through.

It is quite natural for disconnected ideas to race through your mind and strong emotions to fill your heart, for not only your body but your whole being reels from the shock it has received. Usually in time the disturbed ideas fade out and your more rational and logical mental patterns return. But even at the time of crisis it is wise for you to remember that there is a great difference between thinking a thought and doing a deed. So do not feel guilty about some of the thoughts that make a fleeting visit to your mind. They are usually more a reflection of your distress than of your true self.

These uncomfortable feelings and their accompanying ideas can serve a useful purpose. Grief has been called the disease that heals itself. But you must give it a chance by being honest about your feelings. To repress them and to avoid all situations that might stimulate them can cause difficulty in the long run. To acknowledge and express them is healthful, and usually the sooner you do it the better. There is nothing to be ashamed of in having strong feelings. It takes strong people to have strong feelings. They are a valid part of yourself and must be respected for what they are, your honest response to a crisis in your life.

The acute distress produced by untimely death is also apt to show up in your social behavior. If you are one kind of person, you may want to be alone, to see no one. It is almost as if you were trying to claim your grief as your own by clutching it tightly to your breast in solitary misery. Or you may have quite the opposite reaction, even feeling afraid to be alone. You may cling to the people around you for support. Both of these reactions are quite natural, depending on your basic type of personality. Always remember that in the best interests of your future health it is better to admit your feelings and express them than it is to deny and repress them. This means that it is usually good to have other people around who can talk with you about your feelings and help you to express them. Here also you will find that talking with strangers and people of slight acquaintance is often easier and just as useful.

The impact of sudden and unexpected death is most distressing and most difficult to work through healthfully. You will need all the help you can get, and even though you may think you do not want it, it is wise to try to respond to those who reach out toward you in loving concern. They are saying, "I know how much you must hurt deep inside. I would like to help you carry your burden and ease your pain. Please let me try." In ways you may not easily perceive, the help is real and it can ease the pain.

Even when a death has been foreseen for some time it can cause deep distress. The more closely you have been related to the person, the more difficult it is likely to be. The most disturbing losses are usually those occurring in a family — a parent or child, a brother or sister, a husband or wife. Where the fabric of life has been tightly woven together, the rending of the fabric is hard to repair. Major changes in social and family relationships, adjustments in an entire way of life, are called for. Even though you have watched through a long illness or the slow deterioration of old age, the emotional meaning of the change may be more than you had expected. Often a person will say, "I knew he was going to die and I thought I was ready for it, but now it hits me in a way I wasn't expecting." The grief that is anticipated is often quite different from the grief that is experienced. The reason for this is simply that the finality of death shakes the old security system within which one has lived, and now there is the task of finding new ways of making life secure.

Even when there has been time to adjust to the possibility of death, there are emotional reactions that come with the final event similar to those resulting from sudden and untimely death. Here again it is important to accept your feelings for what they are, a valid part of yourself. Only then are you in a position to work through the emotional distress to a mature and balanced readjustment.

There are also times when death comes as a friend to release a feeble existence from intolerable burdens. We see this often with the aged and infirm. A person may be in a nursing home with complete loss of memory and multiple physical complications. Medical treatment may seem to be more a process of prolonging the dying than of preserving meaningful life. The person we have known in his fruitful years has already ceased to be, even though the organic processes of physical existence persist as a distorted echo. When death finally comes under these circumstances we quietly say, "It is a blessing. He really hasn't had any life that meant anything to him for a long time." Then we gather about to pronounce a benediction upon the final episode of a process that had been in progress for an extended period.

Yet even while recognizing the friendly nature of death, we can be filled with another form of sadness, a quiet grief that knows things will never again be quite the same. And we are aware of the sobering fact that we too are mortals who must eventually die. In the death of another we not only foresee our own death, we actually die a little ourselves. For what has been happening deep inside us as we confront death is actually a fracturing of our extended self. The self that is within us is made up of the self that is projected in many directions. It is not just that we relate to other people; in a way we live in these other people. We feel with them, and they feel with us. The deepest experience of life grows from these relationships that are the extensions of our own being into the life that surrounds us.

When you love someone life is wonderfully enriched, but it is also threatened because you are vulnerable to injury through those you love. You know how this works: If you love someone and something good happens to him, you feel good. If something painful happens to him, you feel the pain. If something destroys him, you feel destroyed. Your grief is the feeling that emerges when you feel

5

the pain of emotional amputation, when someone who was an important part of your life is cut off by death. The more your life is bound up with another, the more vulnerable you become.

This idea of emotional amputation presents what at first appears to be a distressing dilemma. We do not want to live as hermits. How impoverished life would be if we retreated from the experiences and relationships that fill it with love and warmth and wonder. Yet we do not want our lives irreparably injured by grief that cannot be resolved. But these are not the only alternatives. We can have the deep satisfaction that love brings to life, and we can survive the threat that comes to life by death — because we are able to mourn.

The ability to mourn may not seem to be a major asset in life. Yet as one of the Beatitudes puts it, "Blessed are they that mourn, for they shall be comforted." In the Phillips version it reads, "How happy are those who know what sorrow means, for they will be given courage and comfort." A wise nature and spiritual resources together make it possible for us to face the emotional amputation of death and emerge from the experience as wiser and stronger persons.

How is this possible? First we should be clear about the way we use our words. *Bereavement* denotes an event of loss in our personal history. *Grief* is the reaction triggered by the event of loss. *Mourning* is the process of restoring inner balance to the person who has suffered loss. Mourning can give back to a person the part of himself that was apparently lost through the death of another.

A healthful mourning process can not only relieve the pain of loss but help you to withdraw the emotional investment you have made in the life of the person who has died. In effect, it is the reclaiming of emotional capital so that it can be reinvested where it will continue to bear fruit in creative living.

One of the mysteries of grief and mourning is that a person who is so devastated by loss that he does not feel he can go on another day is somehow able to discover resources and inner strength that enable him later to look back on the experience of death as a "forgotten pain." The blessed memories will be retained, but the intolerable anguish will have faded away.

In our exploration of the experience of loss we will be seeking to discover the insights and skills that make it possible for you to emerge from the painful encounter with death into new life that is soothed, sustained, and enriched.

This is not an easy process, and we have no magic words to dispel your sorrow. But there is much insight from the past that can be useful in the present. The grief experiences of others can help us to manage wisely our own grief. We can find help and understanding among those around us who have been through the experience of acute loss and have learned how to meet it. We can learn skills and develop inner resources. Any skill or discipline is developed with concentrated effort. To this task we direct our energies in the pages ahead.

2.

Not All Death
Is the Same

The death we encounter is an external fact. The emotional response we have to it is the internal meaning. To develop an understanding of death we must understand as much as we can about how we develop our internal meaning for the external event.

We have spoken of death as producing what we called an "emotional amputation" in the bereaved person. Taking this as a point of departure for exploring the meaning of grief, an imaginative young woman named Marianne Simmel, of Brandeis University, interviewed physical amputees about their experiences. She thought that grief might be comparable to the "phantom limb phenomenon" experienced by many persons who lose an arm or leg. They continue to have feelings in the part that is no longer there. For instance, a person who has lost an arm will often report that he has acute pain in the hand that is no longer a part of him.

When Marianne Simmel interviewed young children who had been born minus a body part she found no evidence of the "phantom limb phenomenon." She interviewed other children who had lost a body part due to accident or war and again found little or no reporting of the experience. With adults who had had a gradual withering away of a body part, or others who had undergone a number of operations that led to gradual surgical removal of more and more of a limb, there was no significant evidence of the phenomenon.

Where she found phantom limb experiences in significant numbers was among persons who had lived long enough to integrate a body part into their total life function, and where the loss of it was sudden and unexpected.

If we draw insight from this study for our understanding of grief it tends to point up two factors. First, the degree of relationship is a vital element. How well you know a person and how long the relationship has existed are important in determining the degree of loss felt. Second, the sudden, unexpected, and acute nature of the loss appears to affect the emotional response. If you have time to prepare and brace yourself you can cope more readily than if you are surprised and caught off balance by the event. In a sudden loss your total system has had no chance to marshal its defenses and feels the full brunt of the emotional blow.

Marianne Simmel's study went on to show that people who accepted the fact of the amputation were the ones who more quickly adjusted to the loss. They learned more rapidly how to use an artificial limb and to get on with the tasks of living. On the other hand, those who wanted to deny their loss, who felt sorry for themselves and rejected the change that had come about were retarded in their progress toward rehabilitation.

If you have known a person for a long time and your lives have been closely related by a variety of common interests you quite naturally feel a greater emotional amputation. A few weeks after her husband of thirty-two years had died quite unexpectedly, a widow said to me, "The hardest part of all this is the thousand and one little things that never seemed important before. Now they are exaggerated out of all proportion. I find myself waiting for the garage door to roll up when he comes home in the evening. I wait for him to turn on the TV news. I start to speak to him across the dinner table. I wake up at night and wonder why he isn't snoring. It's things like this that are hard to take. I know he's dead and I can handle that big fact. It's the thousand little things that made up the real part of our life together that hound me all the time. When will all this stop? When will all of me know I'm a widow?"

What she was essentially asking is how long the grief equivalent of the "phantom limb phenomenon" lasts. With a widow it can continue to be a part of life that decreases only gradually, sometimes

9

lasting several months. It is not unusual for remnants of these feelings to persist for six months. It is a long, slow process that gradually disentangles the fabric of lives intimately bound together.

Not only does the intensity of the relationship sharpen the feelings of grief, but also the circumstances surrounding the severance of relationship.

A young woman whose husband had been in Vietnam for eight months received word that he had been killed when his helicopter gunship had been shot down and his body had been destroyed in the fire that followed the crash.

When I talked with her she said, "When he went over I knew this could happen but I tried never to think about it. Now that it has happened it seems so unreal and far away. You know, I just had to get used to not having him around. The difference now is that he won't come back, when before I always had that hope. Now things are different but somehow they don't seem different. There's nothing definite or final about his kind of death. It's like he was and then he wasn't. You know, just like he evaporated. How can it be like that — somebody so important — and then just fades away."

In her halting words she was saying in effect that a loss to be real must occur within a context of reality. It must happen in a way that makes it possible to feel real grief that can be worked through with a healthful mourning process. But death that is far off and unreal leaves an emotional vacuum that can be filled with false hopes and denials. A tragic loss that is close to the context of living and real to the emotions causes a sharp but clean wound that can heal itself readily. But a loss that is remote and unreal may cause a wound that is infected by doubt and uncertainty. This infected wound tends to heal more slowly and may never heal completely.

A father whose son was killed in the Southeast Asia war zone had a difficult time working through his grief because he fought against his own emotional need. He rejected the personal meaning of the event. He said it couldn't be. He was opposed to the war on political, moral, and social grounds. He did not want his son to go. He urged him to claim deferment as a conscientious objector. But his son went anyway. He had been overseas but a few weeks when his Jeep ran over a land mine and he was killed instantly. When the father was told he almost ignored the information to assault verbally the person who brought the sad news. He accused all members of the military of conspiring in a treacherous plot against the weak and the innocent. When the casket was returned home he refused to have a military service, and instead had a private funeral with only the family present. The emotion that would normally have been expressed at the loss of his son was directed outward in anger toward the army, the government, and the life-destroying society. He gave little support or understanding to other members of the family who felt deep grief. He became more and more hostile, trying to substitute resentment of symbolic and impersonal forces for his personal grief. The external event was surely tragic and painful, but because he organized his energy to fight a different battle he postponed the facing of his inner needs until he had become a changed personality and could only work it out with special therapy.

This father was like an amputee who refuses to admit his loss. He channeled his emotional energy away from the task of facing his grief and doing the essential work of mourning.

When we look at the ways other persons have faced their grief we begin to see the differences of the internal response to the external event. Then we are in a better position to understand some of the emotional reactions that we have.

You can readily see that there are some types of death that demand more of you as you try to cope with them. Some death is logical and some death is illogical. It seems to make sense in some wise cosmic plan for an old person who has lived a long and useful life to die quietly and peacefully in his sleep. Our inner feeling for justice does not fight against a death that fits our idea of what is sound.

Quite the opposite is true when death appears clearly unjust and unwarranted. When, for example, a young person who is talented, dedicated, and has the promise of many years of needed and inspired leadership ahead of him is killed by a person whose criminal record marks a life of low purpose and persistent destructiveness, we have to work hard to adjust to the irrational injustice of it.

These two forms of death mark the outer boundaries of our emotional response. These are the extremes of the just and the unjust, the rational and the irrational. Most of the death experiences you

11

will have to cope with fall somewhere between the extremes. But if you are prepared to handle the extremes you can probably manage wisely what falls between.

Dr. William M. Lamers, Jr., a California psychiatrist, was assigned by the court to counsel with unwed teen-age mothers whose children were being placed for adoption. Dr. Lamers found here a type of grief that can throw some light on the different ways we approach loss. He discovered that those young mothers who saw their babies before they were placed for adoption were able to work through their feelings more quickly and with fewer adverse after-effects than those who did not see their babies. His study of a large number of cases also showed that the mothers who saw their babies were the ones who wanted to get married and have children they could keep. They showed fewer symptoms of disturbed emotions and neurotic behavior. But the girls who did not see their babies developed a variety of disturbed emotional patterns with compulsive behavior and a tendency to withdraw from human relations. They did not appear to seek marriage but instead seemed to want to protect themselves from any intense human involvement.

Dr. Lamers explained the different responses by saying that the basic relationship between mother and child is so deep and intense that its reality cannot be denied without hazard. Seeing the child confirmed the reality of the relationship. Then the normal processes of mourning could be employed. Denying the reality of the relationship diffused the disturbed emotions throughout the life of the young mother.

Those who advised the young mothers not to see their babies (a frequent practice in adoption agencies) thought they were saving them from a painful encounter. They did not realize that the choice is not between pain and no pain, but between wisely managed suffering and unwisely managed suffering.

When we are dealing with the deep and important emotions of life, we do not decide whether or not we will feel. Our feeling is inevitable. We have the choice as to how honest we will be with our deep feelings, and how determinedly we will work through them toward a sound and healthful mode of living.

3.

Your

Emotional Needs

When you meet a serious crisis your emotional needs become at once a major concern. We all know that our emotions are a vital and central part of our personality: our experiences of great joy and great sorrow are emotional responses to living. Yet often we have only slight awareness of how our emotions develop and of what we can do to care wisely for our emotional needs.

Like any other part of our being, our emotions have a history of growth. Everything that has ever happened to us has left its imprint. Sometimes one experience brings a powerful emotional impact; at other times we may not be aware of the forces that have slowly but inexorably modified our feelings. If we are to understand and wisely manage our grief we need to know how it develops and how it can be controlled.

At the beginning we must be aware of the fact that grief is a capacity for deep feeling that lower forms of life do not share. It is only as our highly evolved capacity for meaningful relationship is achieved that we are able to grieve.

Those who have studied the nature of pain indicate that it is a characteristic of highly specialized nerve function. For instance, a clam could not have a toothache. The clam's primitive life-form with unspecialized function has no place for teeth or the miseries that sometimes come with them. So in order to have the privilege of a toothache we must possess the highly specialized form of tissue growth that we call teeth. This is equally true of the whole variety of specialized higher functions that go with being a human being.

So your capacity to have deep feelings for another person is also the source of your capacity for acute pain at his loss. The fact that this capacity is proof of your highly developed nature may not make your grief less painful, but it can make it more acceptable and understandable.

Your grief, then, is not something to be ashamed of or something you should try to hide, for it is the other side of the coin of love. As you are able to love greatly so also you can grieve deeply.

So it is not our capacity for normal grief that should distress us. Rather, it is the tendency to pervert or deny our grief that should be the source of concern. How does our basic capacity for healthful grief get directed into unhealthy channels?

Part of the answer lies in the long, slow process of our learning about death and grief. Many of the more important things in life are not subject to formal education. We can take courses in reading, writing, and arithmetic in school. But where do we learn about love, the meaning of life, and the facts of death? In these areas our learning is usually both indirect and informal. So sometimes we are not aware of the fact that we are learning about these things, because our learning is not specifically identified for what it is.

What is your first memory of death? Is it a thought or a feeling? Was it the death of a neighbor, a pet, a relative, perhaps a grandparent or a great-grandparent? How did the adults around you react to the death? Did they talk in whispers? Did they remain calm and ready to answer all your questions? Or did they divert your questions and act as if the whole subject were taboo for you?

It could well be that you learned more than you realized about death from these early experiences. Even though the subject may not have been openly discussed, you may have learned to associate fear, suspicion, and anxiety with death. And when death occurs even now you may fit these early emotions to the subject as if they were ready-made.

Perhaps an extreme illustration will make this type of informal and indirect learning clear. A fine young man was planning to become a pastor. He had completed college with high honors and nearly finished his seminary training. He came to me one day and said, "I think I am going to have a problem in my parish work with funerals."

I asked him why he felt that way and he answered, "When I see a hearse I break out in a cold sweat. I am afraid to walk past a funeral home. I get upset when people mention death. I just think I'm going to have trouble in my parish with death and funerals."

I asked if he had ever had any distressing experiences with death. He said that he had never been to a funeral and as far as he could remember had never had anything to do with death. Then I asked if his mother was alive and he said that she was. When asked about his father he quite casually commented that he didn't remember his father, for he had been less than two years old when his father died. When I asked how his father had died he said that he didn't know because he and his mother had never discussed it.

Here was an only child of a widowed mother for whom the death of the husband and father must have been a most tragic event. Yet it had never been mentioned. But imagine what must have gone on in the mind of a child that played with other children who talked about their fathers and must have asked about his. Surely the death of his father must have filled his early life with a diffused anxiety that touched nearly everything he thought and did. Yet he could not cope with it because his mother tried to protect him from suffering.

When I suggested that he go home and talk with his mother about the whole matter he agreed. When he returned he said it had been a wonderful experience and that he felt he knew his mother for the first time in his life. He reported that they had stayed up all night talking and that all of the barriers of restraint and repression built up through the years came tumbling down. Two people who needed each other greatly finally found each other. And as time passed he found that his fear and anxiety about death and funerals gradually faded away.

This young man had not been able to meet his emotional needs because of his mother's mistaken idea of protection. One cannot be protected by silence against the harsh realities of existence. The best protection is always a chance to develop a skill in coping with even the painful experiences of life. What might have been a major hazard to his life-work was resolved at the point where he was able to face the facts of his own life and belatedly complete some of the "unfinished business" of his childhood.

Most of us learn about death more openly and honestly. We meet it in the context of our living and gradually grow to have some competence in dealing with it However, if we can be more clearly aware of our emotional needs, we will be in a better position to meet them wisely.

As we try to understand and meet our basic emotional needs in the crisis of death, three things are of primary importance. The first is the need to face reality. The second is the need to accept our feelings. The third is the need to accept help in doing the work of mourning.

One of our ready defenses is to deny painful reality. If we have a severe physical pain we can faint and blot out our conscious-ness of it. When we have a severe emotional pain we can marshal our mental and emotional resources to deny it. When we talk with a person who has just received shocking news, he will often say, "I can't make myself believe it" or "It can't be." This is denial at work. Or he may say that he doesn't want to go to the funeral or see the dead body because, "I'd rather remember him as he was." This too is denial because the simple fact is that he is *not* the way he was. He is dead now and that is the new reality that must be faced directly.

Specialists in the management of grief say that it is essential to break through the denials and face the painful reality before we can begin the healthful work of mourning.

It is possible for us to know the meaning of words intellectually but to reject their meaning emotionally. For instance, the doctor may come into the waiting room in the hospital and say, "I am sorry to have to tell you that your mother didn't survive the operation. Her heart stopped beating and she died in spite of all the emergency actions we took." Intellectually you may know the meaning of all of the words. You may even know what they mean when they are all put together. But to accept the full meaning emotionally, with all of its impact upon life, is quite a different thing. It takes time and a slow process of adaptation to bring all of your being into accord with all the facts.

This brings us quite naturally to the second of your emotional needs, the acceptance of your own deepest feelings. We are led to believe that there is something brave about denying feelings. "Brave boys don't cry." "Be a good girl and stop your crying." But there are times when it is wise and sound to cry. Crying can release emotional tension and make it possible for us to begin to face reality honestly. To take heavy sedation to blot out feelings is usually unsound, for it tends to postpone the feelings rather than remove them. And usually the postponement is to a time and place where they will not be as acceptable or as appropriate as at the time of your initial confrontation with the emotional event.

If you remember that it is a good rule to be kind to your own feelings and equally kind to the feelings of others, you will usually be on solid ground. Because your emotions are an especially important part of your grieving self, they need special consideration when they are most exposed or disturbed. If you understand that this is true of others as well, it will be easier to understand some of the unusual emotional expressions that come at such times.

In addition to facing reality and accepting feelings it is also important to realize that help is available from others. It is also reasonable to accept this help with the knowledge that talking about your feelings and being together with people who understand is an important confirmation of reality and a valid ventilation of your feelings.

No one would say that other people can take the place of the one who has died. That is not the point. But the gathering around you of those who care for you and are concerned about what has happened to you can remind you forcefully that life does continue, that you have a part in it, that you are not alone, and that you still possess much in love and support.

17

Grief is a complex emotion that varies from person to person, for it is a composite of the multiple reactions that make up the life of the grieving person. If we treat it with the respect and consideration it deserves as the other side of the coin of love, the more open and honest we will be about it when death comes. We will be more ready to accept the renewing expressions of love that others offer to us. Geoffrey Gorer, the English anthropologist, has pointed out that we are more emotionally dependent on others at the time of acute grief than at any other time in life with the exception of early childhood. If we recognize the need, we are in a better position to accept and appreciate the help that is available. And also, when we have been helped through an emotional crisis we can understand how important it is to be ready and willing to help others through the crises that occur in their lives.

4.

Overcoming

Cultural Hazards

She was waiting alone at the back of the college chapel. She came toward me with a mixture of timidity and hostility and said, "Why did you let me down too?"

Unprepared for that challenge I said, "I'm sorry if you feel I let you down. Just how do you mean that?"

She went on: "I came to hear you because I thought from the announced subject that you would talk about death. No one will talk to me about it. My best friend was killed in Vietnam. We were in love. Now everything is so empty and I can't find anyone to talk to about it. His family treats me like an outsider. My friends just avoid the whole matter. My roommate says I shouldn't be morbid. Isn't there anyone who cares about me and how I feel?"

Her question and her feelings were real and touching, her need was great. She typified the situation of many who want to cope with their feelings but seem to be denied help. It is not a direct denial so much as an implicit conspiracy of silence. We talked together for an hour but it was far too little to meet a need so great. She had gone through a life-shattering experience and seemed shut off from the type of communication she needed to help her through it.

How skillful we are in coping with death is determined at least in part by the attitudes toward death in our culture. That culture has influenced us in subtle ways often more powerfully than we realize because the influences are unexamined and we do not see clearly what the cultural attitude has done to shape our ways of thinking and feeling.

A young girl can find no one with whom to talk out her grief at the death of her soldier friend in Vietnam. You may have difficulty breaking through a shell of artificial acts and attitudes that surround you in your grief. It may seem to you that everyone is moving about like actors in a play, performing roles but not being their true selves. How do we get beyond these frustrating barriers? How do we break through the restraints that seem to be placed upon real feelings and their expression? Where do we start?

We start with you as a part of your culture. You are apt to share the special feelings and attitudes of your time and place in history.

Attitudes toward death change from century to century, even from generation to generation. How you approach death is probably quite different from the way your great-grandparents did. It is not because someone all at once decided that things should be different. Rather, it is part of the complex movement of life that significant changes, recognized and unrecognized, continue to occur as a result of multiple interacting forces.

You live in one of the most violent periods in human history. Our century is not yet over but already more millions of innocent people have been killed by war, crime, or sudden accident than ever before in history. We don't usually stop to think about this painful fact. We adapt and adjust to our times because we are part of it and close to it. But part of that adaptation has been to protect ourselves against the honest facing of violence and death. One of the psychological defenses we have developed is to block off what is too painful to confront. So we try to stop thinking and talking and feeling about this large area of human experience.

If you find it difficult to talk about death you are not much different from countless others who find it disconcerting to face that fact. One hospital where I have lectured has a tacit policy that no funeral coach may come near the grounds. Innocent station wagons are used to remove dead bodies. Similar practices could be listed at length. If you would like to avoid funerals and funeral homes in an effort to deny death, you are like many others in your community and society.

The simple fact is that it is more difficult for us in our day to face death and the feelings that go with it than it has been in the past. How can that be, you may ask, for death has always been the same. The fact of death has been the same, quite true. But the ways of coming to terms with it have changed.

What used to be taken for granted in the context of living has now become remote and unfamiliar. A college president reports that in response to a questionnaire filled out by freshmen, not one had ever been present when death occurred. Death in our day is removed from the context of normal living into specialized surroundings so that we are not apt to encounter it. Thus we are denied the chance to develop personal competence in coping with it.

The changes that have come about with our technologically skilled generation produce side-effects that modify our living. No one decided that death should be made remote from life. But improved medical care and hospital facilities make it a simple fact of life that most people now die only in the presence of nurses, physicians, medical corpsmen or perhaps state highway police.

How different this is from the experience of your grandparents. A century ago nearly all death and dying was done in the context of the home and family. Those who were nearby might not have been technically skilled but they had strong feelings about what was happening to the one they loved. We have moved from the emotionally involved to the technically skilled, and in the process we have produced an impersonal atmosphere surrounding death. Yet most people, when questioned as to where and how they would want to die, said they would prefer to be at home and in the presence of their families.

The changes we observe deny emotional needs to meet physical needs. Naturally, we favor medical progress but we should also be concerned about what happens to people's feelings. When death is removed from the context of life, the event is real but the relationship to it tends to be remote and unreal.

When a powerful event in our emotional life is removed from direct experience something important happens. The real event in an unreal atmosphere separates cause and effect. When this happens we may give intellectual assent to an event that is rejected emotionally. This fractures our response to life and produces confusion. In our confusion we may deny our emotional needs and then deprive ourselves of the resources available to us in meeting the crisis. So many persons do not know what to say or do, how to feel or act.

This fractured approach to reality may lead you to act as if you think unpleasant things will disappear if you do not look at them. We have built-in devices to protect us from more pain than we can take. Or we supplement natural processes by taking our share of the thousands of tons of tranquilizers and pain-killers consumed annually. Because we can blot out our consciousness of pain we tend to assume we have removed the cause of the pain. But this illusion disintegrates, and sooner or later we have to come to terms with what has led us toward sedation.

When the painful fact is death, and the severe pain is grief, there is nothing you can take to kill the pain permanently. You can reduce it temporarily, but ultimately your choice is to become permanently dependent upon drugs or other forms of denial, or to face honestly the painful fact and learn to cope with it. When you acquire skill in facing reality, no matter how painful, you become a stronger person rather than a reduced and inadequate person.

A cultural mood that tends to deny reality works against the basic needs of people. Our affluent culture has denied us some of the slowly learned skills for coping with deprivation. We have usually had so many of the things we wanted that we have had little practice in getting along without them. Because we have not had to learn to do without many of the little things of life, we have not become adept at getting along with more important losses. When death comes we tend to stand psychologically naked before our loss. The large supply of material things cannot satisfy our emptiness at the emotional and spiritual level of being.

The old ties of family and community that at one time gave structure to life have been eroded. People move so often that they pull life up by the roots. The millions who live in trailer parks and city apartments, military establishments and newly developed suburbs, often find that their ever-new environments do not provide the forms of understanding and ways of acting out deep feelings that were once a vital part of home life, largely taken for granted. And persons who have come from other countries and different cultures tend in America to lose the folkways that provided wise and helpful patterns for working through life's crises.

When we do not know what to say or do in an emotional crisis the tendency is to repress or impact our feelings. Then, instead of meeting the crisis openly and creatively, we seek emotional detours and escapes that lead to a denial of reality and a retreat into illusory thinking. When we try to escape things as they are by building a dream world of wishful thinking we create a vacuum that we fill with anxiety. When we cannot focus our feelings and act on them constructively we tend to diffuse them through all of our life. Then our honest fears become paralyzing anxiety that requires special help to resolve. So in effect our cultural denials tend to make us ill and then to withhold the healing resources we desperately need.

The family, once a source of strength and security, has changed in ways that tend to increase the grief problem rather than to help solve it. The large and multigenerational family of years past could spread emotional stress in many directions. There always seemed to be someone with whom you could talk out your feelings. Now the family is typically a single unit consisting of the husband and wife and their few children. They are acutely threatened by death because it is so totally disruptive of the family unit. In the reduced family circle the members are so emotionally involved with each other that open communication tends to be more threatening than in a large family clan. So also the segregation of the old folks in retirement communities and the children's concentration of activities outside the home tend to make the family less useful in meeting emotional crises than it once was.

It is apparent from this survey that our culture often makes it difficult to meet the deep personal needs of people. We still have the feelings, but they are more apt to be repressed than expressed because they seem inappropriate. So we need special help in developing contemporary and acceptable modes for expressing our strong feelings.

Some of the resources that might have helped us most are rapidly falling prey to a cultural breakdown, and especially to increased intellectualization. With a wisdom that was geared to all of life our ancestors developed ways for meeting crises that satisfied physical, psychological, emotional, and spiritual needs at one and the same time. They developed rites and rituals and ceremonies that furnished appropriate and easily understood channels for expressing deep feelings. Through our emphasis on intellectualization we have lost many of these resources. We must either rediscover some of the old ways of doing things or provide new and equally valid means for expressing feelings and working through our grief. Otherwise we continue to impoverish ourselves, possibly to the point where we will lose the capacity to experience deep feelings at all.

Knowledge acquired in the personality sciences makes it possible for us now to understand the meaning of our behavior as we have never been able to in the past. We are able to understand what our needs are in times of crisis. We are in a position to re-evaluate the wisdom of the past and discover new understanding from the researches of the present. With this insight and wisdom we should be able to improve our skills in wisely managing grief and also make available new processes to aid in healthful mourning.

We must all sooner or later face death, in our own lives or in the lives of those we love. Instead of a fearful and cringing stance that shrinks from this human experience, we can become as brave and adventurous as we have been in exploring other new frontiers of our day.

5.

Your Grief

Is Your Own

It may help you to understand what happens within you when death comes if you can perceive your grief as a form of behavior. It is the total response of your total being to a life crisis. The way you act should be in keeping with your own personality. But there are times when we adopt forms of behavior that are not really expressions of our own being because we can't seem to find our own feelings or would not feel right about expressing them as we feel them. This is particularly true in a culture where conformity is so much emphasized. In TV commercials and magazine advertisements we are urged to do as others do, look as others look, even smell as others smell. We do not usually stop to ask who decides the standards to which we are supposed to conform. We simply tend to lose our own ways of doing things in patterns of behavior that are thrust upon us from the outside.

As your grief is a highly individualized form of response to your inner emotional crisis, it is important that it be understood in personal terms. How others say you should feel or act is secondary to the way you really feel and want to act. Your grief should be the authentic expression of yourself and how you feel rather than a stylized form of behavior that others determine for you. If it does not find genuine expression it will leave remnants that will have to be resolved at some future time lest they continue to plague life with inner conflict and distress.

Marilyn was a member of a church whose young minister had definite but uninformed ideas about how death should be met. When her mother died he told Marilyn that if she was a true believer she would not mourn or have an elaborate funeral. 'She should have the worthless body cremated at once and then have a triumphal service, with every effort to make it a testimony of the joy of true faith rather than as a time of sorrow and grief.

Marilyn, upset and looking to her pastor for guidance, went along with his suggestions. But all the while she felt uncomfortable. She was acting in one way and feeling in another. After the service she had the nagging sense that she had been playing a game with herself. She didn't feel as if she had had a service in keeping with her feelings for her mother. She wasn't quite sure why she felt so uncomfortable about all that had happened, but she felt that way nevertheless.

Marilyn's external behavior was in conflict with her internal feelings. It is important for the whole person to move through a crisis with integrity of being. Marilyn was urged to reject the group behavior within which she felt comfortable for something that to her did not feel right. She was asked to reject her true feelings and to assume a role that largely denied the group support she so desperately needed at a time of disturbed emotions. She was asked to act triumphant when actually she felt confused, sad, and in need of help. Seeking an honest mode for expressing her real feelings she was counseled to take a hypocritical stance, to play a role that for her was quite dishonest.

Even in the case of a person with deep faith and a firm belief in the survival of the human spirit, someone who holds that death is merely a change from the physical state to one of pure spirituality, it should be recognized that feelings are one thing and intellectual beliefs quite another. The belief in immortality may sustain life wonderfully, but there is still the feeling of personal loneliness and the basic change in life patterns that call for adjustment. The process of adaptation to change requires that your deepest feelings be accepted and faced honestly.

Just as there are different kinds of death, so there are different kinds of grief. There is, for example, the quiet, deep, and numbing grief that seems to be beyond the reach of the normal forms of relief. A person may want to cry but cannot. He may want to accept help but not be able to. He may want to talk about his feelings but have great difficulty in finding the words.

In contrast another person may have an explosive outpouring of his feelings. He may cry profusely and vent his grief in a flow of words that matches the flow of tears. The person whose feelings come out so readily is often in a better position to work through his grief than the one whose feelings are impacted. Others can understand and share these effusive expressions more easily than the silent suffering of the person whose feelings appear to be so deeply lodged that they cannot break through.

Some of the difference of expression seems to be a part of a person's ethnic background. People whose ancestors have lived in the Mediterranean basin often seem able to pour out their feelings easily and largely get rid of them. In contrast we find that Northern Europeans tend to be more restrained and rigid, to have a tight control over expression of their feelings. This does not mean that they do not have strong emotions or that they do not suffer from their inability to express them easily.

Even within the same family there are personality modifications that affect the expression of feelings. Men tend to be more restrained than women. Outgoing people tend to let their feelings come out where the reserved and introverted tend to keep them in.

With any generalization there are bound to be exceptions, but for our purpose it will suffice to say that group patterns that encourage easy expression of grief seem to be healthier for the total personality than those that reject and repress the deeper emotional responses of life.

So in coping with your grief you have to look at yourself as a unique person. No one else has had quite the same life-experience that you have had. No one else can have your exact feelings. So a first rule to keep in mind in accepting grief and working through it is to remember that it is *your* grief you are concerned about. It is you who must face it, break through the defenses set up against facing it, and come to terms with the reality of the event with full respect for the reality of your feelings about it.

A young couple who had recently been married were close friends of the best man at their wedding. It was a major shock for them to hear soon after that he had committed suicide. They could not imagine that he would have done such a thing. It didn't seem to fit into his view of life. In fact, they organized all of their mental resources to reject a painful and unacceptable reality.

When I went to visit the couple, the young man told me he had gone with his wife to the funeral home and had stood for a while beside the casket looking at the body of his friend. He said, "We couldn't make ourselves believe it until we saw him laid out."

Nothing was able to break through their organized defenses against painful reality like that moment of truth and honest confrontation that came when they faced death directly. Here was the clearly recognizable body of their friend, eyes closed, placed in a receptacle that would never be used for a live body. Here were the quiet and solemn surroundings of the funeral home. Here was the external reality that spoke directly to their denials in a way that nothing else seemed able to do.

For this reason psychiatrists have said that the moment of truth that comes when the living persons face the dead body can be one of the most significant and therapeutically useful parts of the process of coping with death. Until the whole person is willing to face the facts of the change that death brings, it is difficult or impossible to begin the true work of mourning.

Unpleasant and painful as it often is to face reality head on, the choice you have is simple and unavoidable. You either face reality and release yourself from the hold of denial or you go on living with self-deception. As long as you persist in the denials and delusions you are unable to do the work of mourning. And unless you can do the work of mourning you will build your life upon illusory attitudes that cannot stand up as you move into new and demanding situations.

If you are able to break through the denials, you can begin the healthful work of mourning which makes it possible to retrieve the part of your emotional investment which was bound up with the person who has died. When you recover this part of yourself you are then able to bring into your mental life all of the valued recollections of the dead person. These memories can then enrich your life without causing an emotional hazard. It becomes possible for you to reclaim that part of the dead person's life and experience that cannot be taken away by death. You must let go of the false to discover the true. You must be willing to give up what can no longer be held onto in order to have the treasured memories and inspirations that can come from the life of the one you have loved and now lost as a physical being.

Many persons find it hard to understand the process by which they can move from painful grief to the life-restoring mourning. A simple way of expressing it is to say you must go through the emotional equivalent of a Good Friday to be able to have the restoration experience of an Easter. In the drama of these historical events we find a clue to our personal experience as we move through the pain of grief into the new life discovered through mourning.

Our grief makes us aware of the painful fact of separation and loss through death. Our mourning is our personal and private experience of a resurrection. Through it we discover the spiritual dimension of personality, so rich and full of meaning that cannot be obliterated by the biological event of death. The life that has been destroyed by biological forces incident to our physical nature is restored in the spiritual acceptance of a nonphysical extension of life. Just as we must let go of the physical to realize the spiritual fully, so also we must accept our grief with all its distress in order to come to terms with the new reality that can restore to us what death cannot take from us.

Your grief then is not an enemy but part of a process that can move you toward healthful recollection, spiritual awareness, and personal recovery.

6.

Acting Out
or Acting In

We have examined the nature of death in your life and your culture and have looked carefully at your emotional needs and the personal meaning of your grief. Now we are ready to explore the processes by which your experience of mourning works to return you to a new and fruitful dimension in living.

Mourning is a process of restoration. Wanting to be restored to complete and useful life, you will want to understand how you can most effectively cooperate with the restorative process.

Because death has been around for a long time, mankind has learned some basic and helpful ways for working through it. Some of the things men do at times of death may at first seem strange, but when we look at them closely we begin to realize that more often than not they reflect psychologically sound ways of meeting the needs of the whole person, socially, physically, psychologically, and spiritually. The rites, rituals, and ceremonials that surround the event of death are the accumulated treasure of man's discoveries about his emotional needs and how to meet them. Usually this wisdom has been arrived at unconsciously and over a long period of time.

In our day it seems that many persons fail to appreciate the rich and meaningful inheritance that has been passed down to us in the methods employed for doing the work of mourning. Contemporary students of society are beginning to point out to us how these basic and useful ceremonials function.

Dr. Lawrence Abt notes that every culture provides its people with ceremonial patterns for meeting emotional crises. The major changes in life — birth, adolescence, marriage, political and military events, as well as death — are surrounded by ritualized behavior.

Dr. Abt claims that the major value of these ceremonials is that they make it possible for people to act out feelings that are too deep to be put into words. And in acting out the feelings the whole person can be actively engaged — body, mind, and spirit. These ceremonials make it possible for a large group of people to share a common emotional language. No one has to explain about feelings or acts, for all understand the setting and the valid expressions of feeling within that setting.

Yet another value that Dr. Abt mentions is that the usual ceremonials meet needs at several levels of being. Most ceremonials, in our own culture and in others, are built around parades or processionals. Nearly all provide an opportunity for the whole muscular system to be employed in the acting out of deep feelings. At a baptism the parents proceed together to the altar. A wedding has a processional and recessional. At confirmation the candidates parade to the altar. And military and political events are celebrated with full bands and long parades. So also a funeral is a private parade from the deathbed to the place where the body is placed in the earth.

Most of these ceremonials have a variety of formal events as well as informal counterparts, and each has its meaning for those who participate in them. Those who are involved with death and grief act out their feelings in a variety of both formal and informal events. There may be the informal acts where friends and neighbors call and bring in food to sustain the bereaved. This is a giving of life in the presence of death. Then there are the formal acts such as the religious service where a clergyman presides. Each contributes in its own way to reinforce reality, accept valid feelings, and direct thought and energy toward the goals of mourning, which are the return to normal and healthful living.

Every funeral should help those who grieve to accomplish several important things. It should give people a chance to act out

31

their deep feelings in an atmosphere that accepts and understands. It should provide a dignified and acceptable form for disposing of the outward human form in keeping with religious and social practices familiar to the bereaved. It should undergird the experience of death with an affirmation of faith in life and hope for victory over death to sustain the grieving.

And a funeral should encourage the healthful mourning process by confirming painful reality at the same time that it makes it possible to vent true feelings and accept group support.

A funeral should also provide the community with a fitting chance to express its support of the grief-stricken in ways that can be readily accepted and understood. It should offer all in the community a chance to face their own mortal natures with honesty, to do the anticipatory grief work that will strengthen each to cope with death, and to aid in doing whatever unfinished work of mourning may be left over from past death experiences.

When a funeral is arranged so that it fulfills these important functions it can do much to resolve grief and aid the healthful mourning process.

It is relevant here to say a word about the role of the funeral director. We do not enjoy the occasion that necessitates calling him, but when the need comes it is wonderful to have someone to call on who is equipped to meet our needs. When we are in trouble with the law, a lawyer is a great help; when we are ill, the physician is a blessing; when a toothache comes, a dentist is a source of welcome relief. So also with the funeral director, who stands prepared at any hour to respond to the call for help when death comes, for he is a member of an ancient care-taking profession.

The funeral director obviously knows more about death than anyone else in the community. He knows of its impact upon the living because he has given his life to serving the bereaved and easing their burdens. The training of the modern funeral director provides more crisis psychology than is found in the training of any other professional person in the community with the exception of the psychiatrist. While he would not want to pose as a psychologist he is trained to be perceptive of special needs and to be prepared with wise counsel for those who seek it from him. His insight, training, and experience make it possible for him to provide guidance in providing ceremonials designed to meet deep emotional needs.

Geoffrey Gorer discovered in his study of British attitudes toward death that the more ceremonials people participated in the more readily and completely they returned to normal and healthful behavior. The emotional problems in more acute form appeared where people denied themselves, or were denied by the community, the means for acting out their feelings effectively.

Dr. William M. Lamers, Jr., who has studied the psychological significance of funerals, describes them as "an organized, purposeful, time-limited, flexible, group-centered response to death." The funeral is a psychologically sound and readily available resource for acting out deep feelings. Nothing else that we now have available can serve such a useful purpose so effectively.

The community can provide additional resources to help the mourning person toward his complete restoration to useful living. A number of churches have organized those who have come through the process of mourning into groups especially trained to talk with those who are facing the crisis of death. Some have organized retreats where those recently bereaved can go off together to a quiet and peaceful place to participate in group discussion of their experience, and with others find answers to the problems that perplex them and resources others have found useful. Through free and open communication they often are able to gain new perspective on their painful experience and to grow in both understanding and inner competence.

Most pastors are now specially trained in counseling. In the distressing circumstances of life a skilled spiritual guide can open doors of understanding and insight that change personal tragedy into spiritual growth. He can make the wisdom and experience of generations of faith available to you when you need it most.

To appreciate the value of the resources for expression of our grief, it is necessary to be aware of the hazards when we refuse to act out our deep feelings in ways that are healthful. Dr. Abt has a chapter in his book on "Acting In," in which he points out what happens when powerful feelings are denied their normal expression. These feelings do not cease to exist just because they have been denied expression. When repressed they find detours into forms of expression that may be even more disruptive of life. Many illnesses, including ulcerative colitis, diabetes, asthma, arthritis, and even cancer, can in some instances be traced to unwisely managed grief as one contributing cause.

Acute grief that is not well handled may become chronic. Then it places an unreasonable strain on the glands that provide the balance in body chemistry to meet emotional and other bodily demands. When the body chemistry is out of balance for long periods of time it disturbs these mechanisms of the body whose function is to keep disease in check. Much of the research now being carried on in psychosomatic medicine, according to Dr. James A. Knight of Tulane Medical School, is concerned with the side-effects of unwisely managed grief experiences.

To repress your grief, then, is not to control it. If it is pressed down at one point it will explode at another in illness, personality change, or social maladjustment. When you have available forms for wise emotional expression at the time of death it would be foolhardy to refuse to use them, especially when we know that the failure to work through grief in a sound manner can produce psychological and physical distress that disturb life for a long period of time.

7.

Beliefs
That Help

One of the main functions of religion has been to help people face and master the mystery of death. At the core of most religions there have been symbols and elaborate theories and revelations that center about death and immortality.

Faith is made up of three types of positive response in life. Belief is the intellectual assent, conviction is the inward emotional response, and deeds based on belief and conviction are the concrete application. Faith in the spiritual value of human life is an important element in the positive response of the individual to his own experience of life and death.

Dr. Robert Laidlaw, chief of psychiatry at Roosevelt Hospital in New York, says that in his research he found that people who believed in immortality, who had faith in human survival of bodily death, made more rapid progress in psychotherapy than those who did not. This does not prove immortality, of course, but it does prove the effective function of this form of faith in giving purpose and meaning to life.

At the time when life is shaken by the overpowering evidence of man's physical mortality, belief in his spiritual immortality can be especially helpful in sustaining life. Such an intellectual commitment may be based on many kinds of argument. For example, some hold that if God is ultimate cosmic reality, infinite and eternal, he would violate his own nature if he participated in his own self-destruction, for in endowing man with spiritual consciousness God made man sensitive to something within his own nature that is infinite and eternal. When God made man in his own spiritual image, he guaranteed man's immortal nature, for it is inconceivable that God would destroy himself or even a part of himself.

There is also an ethical belief that supports the basic premise of immortality. It does not seem logical that God would create a being with spiritual sensitivity and then leave this spiritual sensitivity stranded in a universe unconcerned for its highest level of creation. As spiritual sensitivity is the highest form of creative achievement we know of, it then seems logical and right that it would not be singled out for destruction.

Science tells us that in the material realm nothing is ever destroyed. Energy may change to what we call matter. Matter may be changed to energy. Physical bodies change their state but in the economy of nature nothing is lost in the process. Burn a piece of paper and it becomes smoke, ash, and energy in the form of heat. Theoretically these elements could be reconstituted into the original paper, for nothing is lost even though it might be hard to retrieve. By a change in molecular action water can become hard enough for us to walk on as ice, or under extreme heat it may become an invisible gas. But it is all there waiting for those changes that can bring it again into our sensory consciousness. And even when we cannot see the invisible gas we have no trouble in believing that it is there. We know that no physical analogy can explain the nature of the spiritual, but it may indicate some directions that our minds can follow in their explorations.

Science tells us also that there are realities well beyond our senses. Our capacity to see is bound by the colors of the spectrum from red through violet. But we know from the sensation of heat that there are slower-moving red rays that we call infrared. And we can tell by focusing them on certain minerals that there are ultra-violet rays that move faster than our eyes can see. There is reality beyond our senses that we can discover by science or common everyday observation. A dog can hear sounds we are not attuned to and detect faint odors we are not aware of. All about us

36

there is reality beyond our capacity for sense perception. We would not think of denying that reality because of the quite obvious physical limitations we find in ourselves.

Similarly we would not deny spiritual sensitivity just because there are things that are beyond the consciousness of many of us. Students of parapsychology continually explore the phenomena of consciousness that are to many of us forms of awareness resembling the dog's sense of hearing or of smell.

One area of research central to parapsychology has to do with the evidence of mental activity apart from the physical body in space and time. Under laboratory-controlled conditions it has been possible to demonstrate that at least a portion of human consciousness can function beyond the convenient measurements of space and time. This indicates a capacity for what could be called an independent life of some dimension of being beyond the body.

In recent years science has been increasingly concerned with phenomena that are extra-sensory. Much research now is devoted to particle or nuclear physics rather than the mechanics of Isaac Newton. Newton was interested in classification first and individuality second. His approach to classification was through the physical senses and so immediately limited to the three-dimensional framework of physical perception. For instance, Newton saw an apple drop and postulated the force of gravity working on the apple to explain its fall. Most of us have grown up with this kind of approach to both our senses and the physical science postulated and limited by them.

We have to shift our mental gears to begin to understand the new scientific point of view. Modern physical theory is primarily concerned with phenomena that are not within the range of our sensory perception. It is also concerned with individuality first and classification second. The individuality of particle physics involves dimensions of awareness that are more akin to the mystic's consciousness than to the data accesible to our limited sensory equipment.

As some modern scientists see it, the concept of immortality, as that which is essentially beyond space and time is built into the structure of creation. The notion of death is derived from our sensory perception and a Newtonian concept of reality built on ideas of space and time that are now rejected as inadequate by the new physics. In the light of contemporary physical theory, immortality is the rule and death is the exception that proves the rule, for in death men appear to move from the three-dimensional existence of their physical life to a fourth-dimensional existence that has already been a part of their spiritual life. The mystical vision, so much a part of most religious traditions, gives a view of ultimate reality quite compatible with that of the contemporary physicist. At this point, it seems that religion and science may be coming together in a new and deeper belief in the indestructible nature of the individual consciousness. Perhaps our century is the first one in history with the intellectual equipment to understand the revelations of faith about the meaning of immortality.

Our Christian faith was built on the premise that the nature of man had something indestructible at its core. If we try to understand the New Testament revelation we come face to face with this central belief repeatedly. The language was not always precise and the terms could be confusing, but the awareness was sure.

St. Paul, for instance, speaks of immortality. He says, "This mortal shall put on immortality." But he also speaks of the reality of the two natures, "the physical body and the resurrection body." Often in the past men have felt they had to make a choice between a belief in immortality and the concept of the resurrection.

Modern science may well give us a clue to resolve this dilemma. In facing large new concepts with conflicting evidence, modern science often concludes that it is not a matter of "either/or" but of "both/and." Often we have made choices that eliminated important aspects of ultimate spiritual reality. But the old choices are no longer necessary, for ultimate reality is too great to be bound by our small distinctions. Rather, it calls for a stretching of our capacity to grasp what is beyond our normal capacities for easy acceptance.

The New Testament revelation demanded that men stretch their understanding to accept new ideas of the nature of God, the nature of the universe, and their own natures. It was not easy to do, but when men in faith accepted the new revelation they found new life.

The mysterious events surrounding the death and reappearance of Jesus to his disciples must be seen in the light of our most audacious faith, not our efforts to limit reality or revelation. Jesus preached a concept of human values established by a basic and inseparable relation of the human spirit with God's spirit. He claimed "I and the Father are one." This was an integral and indestructible relationship. He also said that he came to give to others "the power to become sons of God." He assured his hearers that "greater works than these shall ye do." He appeared to believe in the basic and essential capacity of man to realize his oneness with God through the achievement of spiritual consciousness. As eyes make no sense without light, and ears make no sense without sound, and lungs make no sense without air, so spiritual consciousness without the relationship with God that fulfills that consciousness makes no sense. He lived and taught and practiced that belief.

Jesus was executed. His body was buried. But then something of major importance occurred. We need to look at the New Testament record closely. Something about him did not stay dead. He went through doors without opening them and that would test one's usual capacity to believe. But his presence was so clear and real that the disciples became changed men. Instead of running in fear they stood firm in their newly discovered faith and challenged the power of the Roman Empire. They changed the world. If we look at history in terms of cause and effect we find the change in the disciples was caused by the powerful impact of the spiritual revelation that came to them in the appearance of Jesus and the indwelling of the Holy Spirit.

The basic fact was that the disciples' concept of ultimate reality was changed from a limited dependence on their five senses to an unlimited ability to understand the power of a resurrection that could prove to them the power of God at work in human consciousness so powerfully that it was beyond biology or physiology. As the mystical consciousness is enmeshed with the fourth dimension, or the spiritual nature, so the power of the resurrection makes clear to man that he is not bound to the physical but at the core of his being is a spiritual being who for a time uses a physical body but is not eternally bound by it. This is quite different from believing that we are essentially physical beings who develop a temporary or tenuous spiritual consciousness.

Yes, the disciples became changed men when they accepted this major new idea about themselves and their empowering relationship with God. Seen in this light the resurrection experience need not be just an event in past history. It can become the point where you discover the meaning of your immortality and the validity of the immortality of those you have loved and who have moved from the physical form of existence to the purely spiritual.

Biblical faith has challenged man to believe courageously and to hope with a hope that is not bound to what is destructive but, rather, by what is creative in life. Paul, who suffered much, also learned to live with a hope that glorified life. He said (according to RSV):

Blessed be the God and Father of our Lord Jesus Christ, the father of mercies and God of all suffering, who comforts us in all afflictions so that we may also be able to comfort those who are in affliction, with the comfort with which we ourselves are comforted by God. For as we share abundantly in Christ's sufferings, so through Christ we share abundantly in comfort too. If we are afflicted, it is for your comfort and salvation: and if we are comforted, it is for your comfort, which you experience when you patiently endure the same sufferings that we suffer. Our hope for you is unshaken; for we know that as you share in our sufferings, you will also share in our comfort (2 Cor. 1:3–7).

But we know that all things work for good with those who love God, who are called according to his purpose. For those whom he foreknew he also predestined to be conformed to the image of his Son, in order that he might be the first-born among many brethren. And those whom he predestined he also called; and those whom he called he also justified; and those whom he justified he also glorified (Rom. 8:28–30).

More than that, we rejoice in our sufferings, knowing that suffering produces endurance, and endurance produces character, and character produces hope, and hope does not disappoint us, because God's love has been poured into our hearts through the Holy Spirit which has been given to us (Rom. 5:4–5).

Here the revelation of the New Testament speaks in clear and certain terms. Man's spiritual nature is of God and therefore as infinite and eternal in its personalized manifestation as God is in his unlimited cosmic nature. Jesus tried to make this clear to his disciples and it was not until he had gone through the experience of physical death and manifested himself in spiritual form that they finally got the message. But when they did it changed their life. It gave them a new awareness of their own inner natures which removed fear and uncertainty. They were still men but quite different men.

As you face death with all of its impact on your feelings and your way of life, the greatest force for sustaining you and bringing meaning to the apparently meaningless, is your ability to see life not with physical preoccupations but in the light of the New Testament revelation. Physical change can be painful and put stress on life. But the insight that moves from the temporary to the permanent, from the physical to the spiritual, from the fear-full to the faith-full can stabilize life.

You are sad, to be sure, but your sadness is for yourself and your feelings of loss and loneliness. This sadness is not rooted in despair. It, rather, is surrounded by the sustaining belief that beyond the physical experience of death there is the spiritual experience of an indestructible awareness of God and his purpose. In that sustaining relationship all of life discovers new and important meaning, and death becomes a more tolerable incident in something infinitely greater.

8.

The Healing
Community

You are a social being. Your life has developed in a variety of groups — your family, your school, your church. Most of the things you have learned, your language, your social customs, your attitudes and practices, are learned through groups. Because they are so important in your development, they become especially important when your life is under stress.

You have no doubt observed that when you are with a group that knows you well and accepts you easily you feel relaxed and comfortable. In contrast, when you move into a group where you are unknown, unaccepted, or uncertain, you feel threatened. It takes mental and emotional energy to adjust to the stress of being in a group that has not made you feel comfortable.

Some of your discomfort grows from your own past experiences. As a child you may remember going to a new school. The first day it was strange. You did not know the teacher, or the other children. You did not understand what was going on around you. But after a while the strangeness gradually wore off and within a few days you were a part of the group and quite comfortable in it.

When you moved into a new community or a new job you probably had some of the same feelings. At first the unknown and the uncertain threatened you. But after you became accustomed to new people and new surroundings you were able to become a part of the life around you and things appeared entirely different.

Erik Erikson tells us that an emotional crisis usually is precipitated by one or more of three conditions, all of which modify a comfortable group relationship.

First, there is the loss or threatened loss of someone who is important to the course of your living. The loss or the threat of it can come about in many ways, the most obvious being death. This is a major event that calls for changes that can certainly make you feel threatened and uncomfortable.

Second, there is the introduction into your life of new and significant people who may make you feel threatened and uncomfortable. A new school or new job would involve this. Sometimes death brings onto the scene new people that you have to cope with in new circumstances, and this can be distressing. The funeral director, the hospital staff, the clergyman all want to be helpful, but the new relationship to them calls for adjustment.

Third, there is the change in status and role relationship. When death comes you have to assume new responsibilities and take on new duties. You may not have been prepared for these changes, and being thrown into them without warning may create a crisis.

The coming of death to one close to you is unusually difficult in that it tends to bring all of these causes for emotional crisis together at one time. A tumult of external changes can be distressing when you feel so injured inside yourself.

It is at this point of convergence of critical events that you can feel the value and the healing power of a redemptive community. You come to it with your needs and in turn it gives you support, understanding, and insight to help overcome the pain and discomfort. You find that you are not alone but, rather, a part of a sustaining group that continues to share your feelings and help you carry your burdens.

Of course, the family should be the primary group for close and healing relationships. The family has been the most continuous reality through your life and its relationships have deep emotional roots. Here you should be able to be yourself without restraint because everyone in the family knows you as you are. So in times of crisis the family comes together from near and far for the purpose of bringing mutual support from those who understand and share your acute feelings.

But sometimes the family already has more stress than it can tolerate and the overburdened small unit needs support. Especially in a small family the feelings may be so intense that everyone seems to add to the tension and each individual may feel that he is "being rubbed the wrong way."

When this begins to happen it is important to recognize the value of wider resources. Even persons who are strangers can be useful at the point of sharing feelings. Casual acquaintances, the butcher, the bus driver, the mailman, all can become important as you talk out your feelings as part of your effort to adjust to the critical changes that death brings. In fact a recent study of widows and widowers revealed that most felt more at ease speaking with strangers than they did with members of the immediate family.

This is one of the reasons why a private funeral can be an unfortunate choice. It reveals a limited understanding of the function of the funeral and of the need for group relationships that are healing.

In our Christian tradition the funeral is a time for worship and for affirming faith. A tragic or threatening event can shake faith temporarily. The bereaved need the support of those who gather around to say that while tragic events do occur in life the long-range faith is still valid and vital.

The private ceremony denies the basic nature and purpose of Christian worship by limiting the chance for therapeutic communication. The immediate family which feels the major impact of the event needs an outgoing expression rather than an ingrowing emotional state that tends to amplify itself.

The best place for the funeral of a loyal Christian is in the church where his faith has been nourished and affirmed. While there may sometimes be other factors to consider such as a type of architecture not suited to a funeral service, or an aged person whose small circle of friends might feel lost in a large sanctuary, the house of worship is the best location for a service that celebrates the worth-ship of life and the importance of the worshiping group in sus-taining the faith of its members.

The funeral service in the church gives an opportunity for forms of expression that are not easily provided elsewhere. It makes it possible to sing together the great hymns of faith. The hymn takes the dormant creed and brings it to life with the stately and stirring tunes of traditional church music. While even fine soloists may stir up the tender feelings, the qualities of the great hymns sung by the congregation tend to confirm the awareness of the supporting group. Such simple forms of support tend to strengthen life rather than to stress its weakness.

The music of the organ, normally associated with the experience of worship, may in distressing circumstances speak in a special way to your thoughts and feelings. It quietly tells you that you are in a sanctuary of God, protected by your faith and supported by those who share it.

Worship uses words that have a healing value. Beautifully expressed ideas that employ traditional and familiar language speak directly to deep needs. The great words of faith in Scripture have a heartening impact in a time of crisis.

Worship gives a chance for meditation. You are invited to be alone with your own deepest thoughts at the same time you are supported by a group of people who are doing their own form of deep thinking. The best of individuality and the best of group life are encouraged in the act and art of worship.

Worship invites your active response through various forms of participation. You can share in the listening, singing, meditation, deep thinking, and prayerful focus of attention. Prayer is simply the form of communication where we pay undivided attention to God. In the midst of the worshiping community you have the chance to become with God's help your own most competent self. In the time of emotional crisis the process of worship can make a vital contribution to the work of healthful mourning.

Talking with the person who conducts worship is important.

Your pastor carefully prepares for the special service because he is sensitive to your needs. He chooses the thoughts and words that speak the special message geared to your problem as he knows it and your needs as he is aware of them.

When you approach this time of worship it is important for you to be alert and responsive. So avoid any use of sedation. You do not want to deny your feelings. You want to manage them wisely. You do that best when you are open to all the creative influences at work around you.

Jesus was sensitive to the importance of group life. He told three perceptive stories that illustrate the various forms of separation from the group and the need for restoration of healthful group relationships.

The lost coin got out of circulation by accident. A lost coin is worthless, for its value is in being used to serve the purpose for which it was created. According to the parable, the woman of the house set to work to find it. She asked her neighbors for help. They looked everywhere and were not satisfied until the lost coin was found. Then she had a celebration, for she rejoiced in the restoration of useful relationship.

The lost sheep probably wandered away because of careless preoccupation with the green grass before its nose. But the shepherd knew the hazards threatening a separated sheep and set out to run the risks necessary in order to bring the sheep safely back into the flock.

The lost son went away in defiance and with deliberate intent. The father suffered over this deliberate separation but he knew that he could not follow along. Rather, he stayed home, prayed and waited for his son's return and the restoration of the relationship. When the son came to himself and returned, poorer and wiser, his father welcomed him with joy and love.

You are always faced with hazard when separated from the group, whether the separation is accidental, like the coin, or due to carelessness like the sheep, or intentional like the son. In each instance the hazards are overcome by persons who are concerned enough to reach out in helpfulness and love. The end result in each instance is restored relationship and the kind of significant communication that helps you to grow through and beyond the hazardous experience.

When you have been faced by the life-disrupting encounter with death you are unwise to shut yourself off from the healing, redemptive community. You show understanding of your own needs and your personal crisis when you strive to keep open the channels of communication essential to the work of mourning.

Similarly you should work to enrich your relationships and group life. Try to avoid the little family bickerings that can compound emotional stress. Your heightened sensitivity could make you vulnerable to hurts and injuries that grow from misunderstandings. Protect yourself by working to enrich your meaningful relations with the group around you. As you try to understand others, you will find that they understand you better and you comprehend yourself and your feelings more adequately.

Then you will accept the help of the healing community and become mature, mellowed, sensitive, a healthy person who is able to help heal the hurts of others.

9.

Children

Feel Too

The healing community is a resource for you. But you, too, are a part of the healing community for others around you.

This may be especially true for children. Often we think children are too young to understand death. We feel grief is for adults only. So we may neglect children when death occurs. But few crises have the impact that death does on children. They have a long life ahead of them and anything we can do to help make the way smoother for them will pay dividends of happiness and release from stress for them for years to come.

Because the life-experience of children is limited, we are apt to discount their capacity to feel grief. Naturally the nature of a child's grief will be different from that of an adult. But its intensity may be equally great and the ways it shows itself may confuse you as an observing adult. It may not seem like grief at all. It may even seem to you to be inappropriate or even inconsiderate behavior. Yet if you look closely at the emotional life of a child and its development you can more readily understand what is happening. Then you will be in a better position to aid the child through his difficult readjustment to loss.

You will probably observe that the child's response to loss varies with his age. The older he is the more background he has and the more facets there will be to his reaction to loss.

Let us start with the very young child. People often say to me, "But he is too young to understand," and I usually respond, "Yes, but not too young to feel."

Feelings are of great importance to the young child because, for the first two or three years of life, he has no language. But if you have had children in your home you know how much they can communicate without using words. And much is also communicated *to* the child without the use of words. The young child lives by his feelings so is naturally very sensitive to the feelings of those around him. If there is a marked change in mood or attitude he senses it. His sensitivity is so great that the emotional atmosphere around may actually make him ill.

You can probably remember little that happened before you were three years of age. If you do remember anything it probably was an emotional event that made you happy or sad. Conscious memory usually begins with the ability to use language, but unconscious or preconscious memory begins with life itself. All the things that have happened to you are stored away in your mind. They have emotional meaning for you even if you cannot remember the events that produced the feelings. A small child undergoing loss or change feels his security threatened. He may show it by changes in his actions. He may not want to eat or play. He may be fretful and easily upset. He cannot know what death is because he cannot understand space or time. But he can feel the loss of a person who is warm, loving, close, and constant in his life.

In treating the grief of a young child it is important to try to supply those things he misses most. He needs extra quantities of tender love and care, emotional warmth and affectionate attention. In other words, the vacuum created by the loss needs to be filled with the best possible emotional substitute.

When a child is older, from four to seven, he can talk about how he feels. But the focus of his talking or active responses will be bounded by his limited experience. He has developed skills in the use of his body. He can run and play. In fact, his interests are apt to be centered about himself, his body and how it works. He is also interested in the bodies of others, how they work, how they feel and why they do what they do. So when death comes into his experience he will quite naturally try to take hold of the event with a focus on his biological preoccupations.

He will probably ask you simple and direct and sometimes distressingly blunt questions about death, but they will be largely centered about its physical aspects. He may want to know what they do with the body. He may ask to feel the dead body. He may want to know why the eyes are closed. He may ask about bodily functions. In all of this he is trying to get a clear picture of what the biological difference is between life and death. He is trying to discover what it feels like to be dead.

It is important for the adults around this child to answer questions as they are asked in brief and simple form. To over-answer the questions would show that you are anxious about the subject. To reject the questions as improper would be to close off communication and surround the subject with mystery and anxiety that is not warranted. It is also important to realize that behind his curiosity there is the same emotional need for warmth and acceptance that the younger child has. Accepting his questions and his curiosity means you accept him, and he is sensitive to rejection at the time of his grief.

When a child is eight to eleven he has moved into a new world of social relationships. He is in school, a community beyond his home. He is a social person. He begins to compare his family attitudes and activities with others in his enlarged community. When death comes into his life, he will have a need not only for warmth and biological answers but also for coping with the social meaning of death.

You will often detect this enlarged interest in his questions. When Johnny's father is killed in an accident, you might be asked, "Who will take care of Johnny now?" This is social concern. Your child may also ask questions about his own security. You can tell what is going on in his mind when he asks, "Would I have to go to a children's village if you were killed?" As far as is reasonably possible he should be reassured. You could say, "We expect to be around for a long time yet. We want to enjoy our grandchildren." Yet even though he may express his concern in social questions, he needs your special effort to be sympathetic and understanding, patient and perceptive.

The older child has a clearer idea of space and time so he can have a more explicit idea of what death means in terms of its physical finality. He may appear to brood and when asked about his thoughts may say, "I wonder what it would be like to be dead." In effect he is telling you that he is trying to grasp the meaning of being and nonbeing. This makes a good starting point for some simple but practical education. We can explain, for example, that we know much about life, and that careful living can prevent many of the accidents that end life. So the apprehension about death can be used to safeguard life and develop responsible actions toward others and in relation to himself.

The teen-ager has a different set of attitudes and interests. At this age the young person is trying to discover the meaning of his own life. He tends to be philosophical in his own way, and experimental with his life. He is aware of rapid and significant physical and emotional changes. He is able to use quite abstract forms of thought and language. He is apt to be preoccupied with the problems and dimensions of his own self-awareness. At the same time his social life is structured by a concern for his group and what they think and do. While he has a great capacity for rational thought he also has tendencies toward irrational behavior.

All of these characteristics of this period of rapid change will have strong bearing on his thoughts and feelings about death. How he will express his feelings may be closely related to the freedom with which you have talked about the subject in the past.

For the teen-ager, death may be a severe trauma and threat. The loss of a parent may fill him with guilt and he may withdraw into himself and struggle alone against the mysteries of life, death, and guilt. He may want desperately to talk with you about his ideas but he may not know how to start or whether you would think it a proper subject for discussion. So he may spend hours thinking his own thoughts. Out of his meditation he may produce insight and growth, or he may dig a pit of depression and fall into it. Here it is well to remember that some of the great poetry on the subject of death was written by teen-agers: Bryant, Millay, and Schubert, for instance. But in our day many teen-agers try to come to terms with death by suicide. The capacity for philosophical exploration is great, but so also is the need for emotional support, valid answers, and sensitive and kindly understanding through the period of stress and readjustment.

Teen-agers have an odd mixture of idealism, self-interest, and impractical behavior. Even the impractical behavior needs to be explored with him to understand what it is saying, for all behavior expresses meaning.

Parents concerned about how hard their teen-age son was taking the accidental death of his best friend invited me to have a talk with him. I found him standing alone on a bridge over a tidal inlet near the harbor. He had a handful of singles and five-dollar bills earned in after-school work. Quietly and meditatively he dropped one of the bills into the water and watched it float out toward the bay. Then he dropped another and watched it disappear. My first reaction was to interrupt this apparently irrational behavior. Then my next impulse was to try to understand it. So I said to him, "Do you know why you are doing that?"

He didn't answer for a while, but then he looked at me and said, "Nothing's worth anything. It all just floats away. Death takes everything sooner or later. I know money isn't worth anything. You know it too if you're honest with yourself."

In effect, he was acting out the meaning of his grief. He instinctively knew that the essential element of grief is the ability to let go of the things that can no longer be held. His was a symbolic action, seemingly irrational but basically profound. At the time of death we often use money symbolically. We give it away or spend it for emotionally determined purposes. He was using it to act out his feeling that nothing, especially material things, is important in the face of death. As far as I know he has never done anything like that since. But at that point it was an important symbolic act for him. Also it was important that it be understood for what it was. To have ranted at him for wasting money would have been to miss the point and alienate him. To accept it as significant and symbolic behavior made it possible for a deep and traumatic experience to be shared. And it became a point for personality growth.

Three or four simple rules can be helpful for you in facing death with the children in your life.

Try never to deceive a child. It is difficult to do anyway, for children have built-in lie detectors attuned to the emotional overtones of what is said. While they may not detect the details of deceit, they sense the mood of deception. To lie to them at a time of crisis is doubly dangerous, for they are not only deprived of the answers they need to cope openly and honestly with the events of life, but they are also threatened by the feeling that they cannot depend on those to whom they would normally turn for guidance.

Try not to over-answer a child. To give more of an answer than the question requires shows anxiety. You do not want to add to a child's anxiety at any time, but especially when he is facing a major emotional crisis.

Try to include children in as much as possible of the family activity at the time of death. Children will participate as far as they are able to understand. Funerals are an important family event and more children are injured by exclusion than by inclusion in them.

Try never to force a child to do what he does not feel comfortable in doing. Children have been severely injured emotionally by demands like forcing them to "kiss Grandma goodbye." This type of force can be quite brutal and is inexcusable.

Try always to see the events through the eyes of the child, and with the degree of emotional development that is normal for him. Then it will be his feelings that you will be dealing with rather than a projection of your own.

In your patience with the child and your understanding of his special needs you may find that you yourself are being helped to face death with a new openness and honesty. It is quite common for children to help adults at the same time that the adults are helping the child. By sharing your own thoughts and feelings with him and responding to his needs, you and your child can together do a better job at the healing work of mourning.

10.

Meeting Crises
with Skill

We have looked at death and grief from many different angles in the preceding pages. We have explored their personal impact on your body and mind, their social effects, their religious meaning, and the resources for meeting them effectively. In these few concluding pages I want to re-emphasize the importance of your initiative and effort in coping with them. Whether your loss cripples you or furthers your creative growth is largely up to you.

The event of death can be so shattering that we feel helpless before it. In our shock and confusion we may feel powerless to do anything about our feelings or our lives. Without minimizing the overwhelming distress and disruption death can bring, I suggest that you can turn the crisis into an occasion for deeper spiritual understanding and more creative living than you have ever known. You are the most important force in your own environment, the key factor in your future. How you use your inner and outer resources is, finally, up to you.

You may be tempted when the stress is great to give up the very things you need most to surmount the crisis. Job's wife scoffed at his faith and urged him to "curse God and die." But Job persevered in faith even as he protested the injustice of his sufferings, and was led to a deeper understanding of his Lord.

To reject your faith is to place yourself at the mercy of your fears. To give up hope is to open the floodgates to despair. To give

54

up the sustaining power of love is to let in bitterness, resentment, and hatred.

How, then, can we hold onto faith, hope, and love through the crises that challenge them? Most people who have come through a time of stress victoriously have found it a moment for reaching deeper with the roots of faith, the ground of hope and the dedication of love. A tree accustomed to a prevailing wind reaches far down with its roots so that it is secure when the storm blows. The person who works to keep his life firmly grounded in faith not only meets the normal stresses of life with confidence, but when storms come his roots are deep enough to hold firm.

Many who have suffered a tragic event have found it so meaningless and futile and unexplainable that they tended to generalize from it to all of life. This is an irrational response that we must beware of. Because one food made us ill would we stop eating forever? Because we saw something disturbing would we close our eyes permanently? Because we heard painful news would we plug our ears? It makes no more sense to destroy our capacities for trust and wise living because one tragic event came our way.

The death you face is a major event in your experience, one of life's most acute deprivation experiences. But it is not the end of your life. It might even be the beginning of a finer and more fulfilling chapter in your personal history.

Our culture of abundance has not given us much practice in managing deprivation. When we meet a major deprivation experience like death without practice in coping with minor losses, we sense our special need. When we are aware of special needs we tend to reach more vigorously toward special resources.

Some of these resources are within yourself. They are your capacities of mind and spirit. You can control your mind. You can focus your mental activity, your attention, on only one thing at a time. You can choose what that will be. Your choice at this point can largely determine whether your mind will work for you or against you. If you focus on the tragic event it will become even more tragic in its effects on your life. If you focus on your ability to cope with it, it can become a growing experience that will strengthen your life.

Your emotions are also an inner resource. You can use your mental resources to help determine the focus of your feelings. I know this will be difficult at first, but the sooner you start the better and easier it will be for you in the long run. While you should not deny your feelings, you can channel them to enrich your living and your relationship with others. Instead of harboring feelings like bitterness and hostility you can try to become understanding and perceptive of others. Some of the great expressions of social concern have grown out of a tragic event that inspired people to act to relieve the suffering of others. The sinking of the *Titanic* produced an improved iceberg patrol. The tragic illness of a president produced a foundation that has almost completely eradicated polio. You can use your tragic experience to become a warmer, more mellow and perceptive person rather than letting it cut you off from useful living.

Some of the resources are outside of you. But they cannot serve your need without your cooperation. The redemptive community, the church with its ceremony and worship, your neighbors with their interest and concern, your pastor with his skill as a counselor and spiritual guide, your physician with his concern about your physical well-being, your lawyer with his informed interest in the legal implications of major life-changes, and even your government with its social security and other resources for helping you through personal crises — all are waiting to serve your needs. But in each instance you must be willing to be helped and to cooperate.

Life does not always move at the same tempo. Someone asked Einstein once to explain the theory of relativity, and he rather facetiously said that it was like the contrast in the emotional meanings of time: if you sit in the moonlight with your best girl for an hour it may seem like a second, but if you inadvertently sit on a hot stove for a second it seems like an hour. Time is relative to the emotional forces at work during any given period of life. In a time of tragedy the rapid movement of your emotions may make it seem that you have lived more, endured more, and learned more in a few days than in months or years of ordinary living.

In military history we see armies spending long periods in training and waiting. Then comes the brief encounter, and the decision that results from the battle. The hinge of history, as Churchill pointed out, swings on the encounters that are brief in time but important in setting the course of history.

A tragic event is like a battle in your personal history. It is a time of decision and the course of your life may be set by the way you conduct your private engagement with painful reality. You may be defeated by the event and move on into life crippled in spirit and emotion. Or you may emerge from the personal battle with a new and firmer faith, a deeper sensitivity to the needs of others, and a new capacity for concern and understanding.

The strategy of your personal encounter with grief may be determined by the questions you ask yourself. It has often been said that it is more important to be able to ask the right questions than it is to find the right answers.

Your questions represent the growing edge of your life. They determine in large part what your autobiography will be. The questions that begin with the word "why" lead to interpretation, for they are a quest for meaning and purpose. The questions that begin with "how" usually lead toward a quest for skills and abilities in coping with events.

If you ask: Why did life do this to me? you put the tragic event in control and take the initiative away from yourself.

In contrast, if you ask: How can I face this tragic event so that I will grow through it to be a better person? you will be taking a step to keep you in charge of events rather than having them in control of you.

Instead of asking: What is life doing to me? try to ask: What am I doing to life?

Instead of asking: Why is life getting me down? you can ask: How can I lay hold of the resources that will hold me up through this time of stress?

57

When you want to feel sorry for yourself you might ask: Why did this have to happen to me? But instead of moving self-pity into the center of the picture, you could express concern for what the same event has done for someone else and ask: How can I help someone else in this same situation? As you try to help someone else, you will find that you are helping yourself also.

Instead of asking: Why must I endure so much? you could ask: How can I find life's true meaning in these painful events?

If you are interested in sailing you know that the more lead you have in your keel the higher you can raise your mast and the better you can take advantage of the wind by carrying more sail. The more skill you develop in using the strong wind, the more chance you have of winning the race. The same wind that can be used to win a race can drive the unskilled aground.

In the course of life, your faith can be the keel that holds you secure as you lift up a high mast to take full advantage of the resources to meet the challenges life brings. It may not be easy, but the most important things in life are seldom easy. The more worthwhile our experiences and endeavors are, the more important it is to develop the skills, disciplines, and resources to make us personally adequate.

Even the worst of life-experiences can be used to achieve the best of life's response. The cross of Good Friday led to the joyous awareness of new life on Easter. In the face of your tragedy you can find the personal meaning of resurrection.